BIRD RIVER

Bird River

John Davies

First published in: 2023
© John Davies/Carreg Gwalch, 2023

All rights reserved. No part of this publication
may be reproduced, stored in a retrieval system,
or transmitted in any form or by any means, electronic,
electrostatic, magnetic tape, mechanical, photocopying,
recording, or otherwise, without prior permission
of the authors of the works herein.

ISBN: 978-1-84527-937-0

Published with the financial support of the Books Council of Wales

Cover design: Eleri Owen

Published by Gwasg Carreg Gwalch,
12 Iard yr Orsaf, Llanrwst, Wales LL26 0EH
tel: 01492 642031
email: books@carreg-gwalch.cymru
website: www.carreg-gwalch.cymru

Printed and published in Wales

For Marilyn and Ceri

All the bird carvings in the book are the work of John and Marilyn Davies. The photographers are credited under each image.

Contents

Chapter 1: The river   9

Chapter 2: Charles Tunnicliffe (bird painter) and Harold Gill (wildfowler)   13

Chapter 3: John Moore (bird carver), Stan Taylor (bird carver) and Marilyn Davies (bird painter)   19

Chapter 4: The Ward brothers (bird carvers) and Wendell Gilley (bird carver)   25

Chapter 5: From the river   29

Chapter 6: Clyde Holmes (painter and poet) and wood thoughts   35

Chapter 7: Pierino Algieri (photographer)   43

Chapter 8: Poetry by John Davies   49

Chapter 9: Slate carvings; Billy Rice (slate sculptor) and Mary E Thompson (artist)   62

Chapter 10: R S Thomas (poet)   68

Chapter 11: Near the river   73

Acknowledgements   78

John by the Clwyd

Marilyn Davies

Chapter 1: The river

Between Rhuddlan Castle and Rhyl harbour is a tidal three-mile stretch of the River Clwyd whose eastern bank, a public footpath, I walk about once a fortnight not just for relaxation. I carve birds, they need driftwood perches, and there's a rich permanent collection of driftwood here. Especially I'm looking for intricately curved whorls of ivy. But I keep an open mind and eye and never tire of it. A few days after a big storm, when wood's had time to drift downstream, is harvest time.

Bird life is rich here too: shelduck, mergansers, cormorants, snipe, heron are common, and gangs of Canada geese swagger about, supervising. Best I like the shorebirds like sandpipers, redshank and curlew with long beaks that are calling's arcs. A few years ago I saw my first little egret, white emblem of global warming, and pointed it out to a passer-by who doubled my sense of good fortune by regretting that, no, his eyesight wasn't up to it. Once, I heard a mechanical whump-whump sound as, above the river but half-hidden by the near bank, something passed black-white, black-white. I watched baffled – until two swans flew into view, a black and a white.

This is a borderland where the urban meets the rural – traffic on the by-pass flies higher than most swans and geese above the river – around that rare thing in Wales, a big flat coastal plain. (At one time, the western half was known as Little Canada.) There's a caravan park. The police helicopter used to be near the water too. One day I was walking back to Rhuddlan when I met Ray, licensed wildfowler, carrying his shotgun and a Canada goose he'd shot. (Which, says Ray, invariably tastes of river mud so needs a lot of salting.) Suddenly the police helicopter was hovering overhead, keeping pace with us. In the end, Ray stopped, put down his gun and goose and, staring up with arms outstretched – Man challenged by the Machine – gestured 'WHAT?' Off swept the helicopter. That seemed that. At the car park though where police were waiting, Ray had to produce his wildfowler's licence because apparently a swan had been shot. Not so, said Ray always confident: he'd seen the scattered feathers below the telegraph wire it had hit, a common occurrence. Eyes narrowed, town and country braced for a stand-off. Then went their separate ways. My money was on Ray. When he informed me once, bluntly, flatly, that the heron skull flaunted on my workshop wall was actually a cow's nasal passage, I took it down.

Also on this urban-rural borderline I saw a camouflaged hunter with air rifle and dog – and wife/partner stumbling behind him in coat and heels, clutching a handbag ('Come and watch me shoot a rabbit, Sue') like a parody of loyalty. Then there was the small tribe of young men living by the Clwyd for about four months last summer, on a muddy creek at Rhyl. Some lived in a sod hut they'd built, flying a Welsh flag. Some lived in tents. Nearby was a handsome structure made of driftwood and a large bakery tray. By the time I encountered them, they were shooting rabbits and fishing but had decided not to kill pheasants because it was the breeding season. They were jobless. A lot of the money saved on accommodation went on drinking in the scenery. And they left behind, filling two burned-out cars already there when they'd arrived, hundreds of beer cans shining silver against the rust-brown like an Arts Council installation. I admired their enterprise, living, as one of them put it, 'the rock 'n' roll lifestyle'. So when later one of them checked out my armful of wood and driftwood-collecting costume and asked, 'Sleeping rough, are you?', I felt oddly flattered.

I love setting up a piece of driftwood to launch the latest bird. I love the dried-out look of driftwood, the curves that have survived the rush of the river. I walk miles because only about five per cent of what you see is worth collecting. The rest is mostly straight, unusable. The sap in the wood has been sluiced out by the river so the wood doesn't rot. Still, it's wet and I put it in the microwave which has the extra advantage of driving out woodlice. These days I start with the driftwood not with a carving. It should complement the bird. To find out how, I leaf through one of my favourite books, Collins' **Lifesize Birds** or the RSPB's comprehensive **Britain's Birds**. So you have a fine

Little owl

Peter Hughes

piece of wood that curves on itself, looping in miniature versions of – a little owl? I check with my wife Marilyn who will paint the bird, and whose sense of colour is far superior to mine. Ivy is useful because it's so thin, tough and supportive, so light in colour. I use a lot of ivy. But I set myself limits in terms of what changes I will make because the bloom will be easily lost from a piece of driftwood that has been recoloured or reshaped. Sometimes a customer on the verge of buying a bird says, 'I'd like the driftwood – but could I have it more curved/angular…?' Alas, no.

Another customer bought one of my greenshanks from a gallery at Llanrwst and, although cautious ('But what if the beak breaks?') she invited me to view the river driftwood on her estate. How was I to haul the rich harvest home? I needn't have worried because suddenly there it was, a single pile under a tree. The rich are not rich in everything.

The River Clwyd, as far as I'm concerned, is a three-mile storehouse, hurrying to the sea. There are joggers soundproofed against the season; fishermen now and then; the occasional flower-arranger poaches my driftwood. I think of the poet Waldo Williams's comment to the caretaker of a chapel: it was nice enough but small. The caretaker's reply was weighty: 'It's big inside though'. Waldo wrote in a poem 'What is living? To have a wide hall between narrow walls'.

Chapter 2: Tunnicliffe and Gill

Early on I became a fan of Charles Tunnicliffe (1909-79). His painted birds in a series of well-produced books were sufficiently minimalist to entice a beginner to fly, his colours real and muted. Especially invaluable were the measured drawings of birds. I had been relying on measurements of specimens in a museum – hard to believe now.

Early artistic promise on his father's Cheshire farm led to the Royal College of Art. Commercial work followed and breakthrough: in 1932 Tunnicliffe produced the wood engravings for Henry Williamson's hugely successful **Tarka the Otter**. During the war years, holiday visits quickened his enthusiasm – and in 1947 he and his wife Winifred moved to Malltraeth on Anglesey, to a bungalow, 'Shorelands', with a stirring view of the estuary. I've enjoyed many times the view from the Cob, a spacious sea wall built in 1812, staring resolutely down the estuary. Anglesey County Council purchased his collection of paintings soon after Tunnicliffe's death; they are now on display nearby at Oriel Ynys Môn in Llangefni. He was a fine writer too. Here's a flock of golden plovers near Malltraeth (from **Shorelands Summer Diary**) in 1947:

'The birds wheeled about the confines of the field in ever-changing formation, one part of the flock at times seeming to pour down through the other ... On set wings they glided down, then, with a silvery flickering of wings beautiful to watch the host ceased its forward progress and delicately touched ground.'

There's so much to admire here, the surge in the long sentence, the bold verb 'pour', the colours and movements emphasized by the flickering of 'i' sounds in 'silvery flickering of wings'. So the writer conveys his absorption. Tunnicliffe's observant eye is tireless – as when crows ascend vertically, without a wing-beat or when terns use tails and streamers to feed from the waves without a splash. He can be imaginative: a cormorant dives 'as if ashamed'. And how does he know

Little tern

Chris Porteous

that a flock of golden plovers that appeared on April 18 is also the one that passed on April 29?

Dead birds were brought to him – a significant number the victims of sportsmen – and Tunnicliffe noted details of where the bird was found, its donor and the condition of the plumage. Most important were the careful measurements of the specimen. These 'feather maps' as he called them were to help him draw future birds. To me this sort of first-hand information was a great help – up to a point. Early on I was lent a stuffed owl by a friend but the effort of conveying through wood the essence of a balloon overwhelmed me. The owl eyed me doubtfully, creaked on his perch. Under his feathers he seemed eighty per cent air and I turned to a smaller, easier bird. In time I learned to appreciate what the curves of rounded bellies, the cripsness of wings, the variety of head positions can achieve – in Tunnicliffe's hands at least. But the artist had anticipated the woodcarver: 'it would be wisdom to familiarise yourself with the skeleton of the bird first and with the arrangement of the feathers afterwards. For the latter, the study of stuffed birds is helpful, but only for the feather details.' Perhaps the most iconic of all his measured drawings is that of the golden pheasant, produced in 1959. The page is aflame .

One expects perfection. So for this relief much thanks: in the November 2007 Charles Tunnicliffe Society publication, **Reflections**, Eric Hoskins is recorded as saying about Tunnicliffe's bittern: 'There's something wrong with it; the eyes are not right ... A bittern is boss-eyed; you have done the painting mainly from a skin but it was a skin that had not got the eyes in it.' Tunnicliffe took it like a man: 'By God, Eric, you were right.'

For many years I enjoyed the mock-up of Tunnicliffe's workshop amongst his paintings at Oriel Ynys Môn. The table was littered with painter's necessities, a snowy owl was pinned to a table and behind them: a world of sky. It was an honour to have our carvings exhibited alongside his paintings in the Birds of Wales exhibition at Oriel Ynys Môn curated by Jane Huskinsson in September - October 2017.

When we returned from a year in Michigan I was feeling the need to reconnect with north Wales. I found a booklet in our bookshop entitled **Dee Wildfowler**, published in 1982. It was an interview with Harold Gill (1883-1961) of Parkgate on the Wirral, recorded and edited by Leslie Brockbank. Both men were founder members of the Dee Wildfowlers' Club. Gill had spent thirty-three years with his companion Monk Jones shooting birds for the markets of Liverpool and Manchester from a duck punt. On October 10 every year, two to three thousand pink-footed geese descended on the estuary and remained there until March 20. Every year. Mallard, teal, wigeon and pintail were also plentiful. A punt is not flat-bottomed but more like an elongated saucer otherwise the punt would stick to mud like two pieces of wet glass. There is a seven yard recoil on the duck punt.

The nature of the interview is perhaps summed up in this sentence: 'You have to live and think like the birds so you live in the quietude of dawn and that I am sure has an effect on you'. Here is a writer with a claim upon you. He is thoughtful, keen to be understood, possessed. Here are some of his observations: keep your punt steady because wetness glints a warning to the birds. The best shot: at about sixty yards. On water, birds always seem closer than they are. The fouler the weather the better the fowling. Small birds will often perch on the boat when a hawk is about. 'Wigeon are often stupid but they tend to flight later than other birds. This may be wisdom on their part.' In its recording of felt life, its vibrancy, this work had the effect on me of a fine novel.

Some time in the nineties I met Su Walls, an artist living in Pwllheli. I'd given a talk in which I'd mentioned Gill and she came up to say she'd known him as a child. After we chatted awhile I said, 'Look, if I send you a photocopy of my book of Gill recordings would you jot down your reminiscences?' She painted a compelling picture. Mr and Mrs Gill were gentry. Other gentry lived in Neston but not in Parkgate. Alone except for his wife and, especially, Monk, he lived to a code. 'I would never kill birds unless I knew they were for food.' He was an outsider, an engineering graduate doing a workman's work voluntarily. 'I'm no scholar,' he says in language that denies it. Brave, resourceful, he would exercise self-control: 'one member of the party would not or could not stop singing. He sang his head off all through

Wren

Marilyn Davies

a wonderful flight. All of us got a few duck, except for him. Threats that we would shoot him had no effect and he even sang all the way back. I had never known him sing a note before.' Joy should be private, expressed through imagery : 'we punted down there at night and I think we had all the mallard in the river like faces in a theatre stretched along a steep bank.' Says Su Walls, 'He always remained very remote and wonderful.'

Gill and Monk escaped death on several occasions. Once, sailing from Bagillt, they couldn't see a yard in front of their faces with the rain. The fact that Gill and Monk were standing up drove the boat along. Some fishermen were calling them for help but it would have been suicidal to help, turning the boat broadside. One of the fishermen was drowned that night. The most moving part of the interview was this extract:

'Monk Jones was a wonderful chap. You could search England for a better one and he, too, knew no fear. Only once did he say, "I wonder if we'll make it". At the time I felt as uncertain as he did but I replied, "It's a sure thing, Monk".'

Tunnicliffe and Gill are linked in my mind. Englishmen raised in Cheshire on the border, Tunnicliffe slipped across to Anglesey while Gill sailed a duck punt between home and what he knew as the Welsh Side. They were both passionate birdmen yet disciplined. Writing mattered little to Gill, happy to have his life recorded, whereas Tunnicliffe wrote several books, the most valued being **Tunnicliffe's Birds** (measured drawings). They lit up the journeys I've made to their home territories and gave my work as a bird carver momentum.

Chapter 3: Moore, Taylor and M Davies

I'd been living in Provo, Utah, for a few weeks when I was given the name of John Moore, carver of birds and fish. We quickly became friends. It was 1988. He was retired and I was teaching poetry for a year at Brigham Young University. Under a granite mountain which shone pink in the late afternoon, we set about our projects with chisel and knife while the radio played. This went on for a month or two. Then John had a vision (literally: this was Mormon territory) which prompted him to pay thousands of dollars to Franz Dutzler of Oregon for a three-day course in fish-carving. I awaited his return with interest. Was that the roar of a motorbike? He was a changed man. The radio disappeared and power roared in, the Dremel cutting tool. It saved time but at a cost: the new levels of dust and noise involved him wearing a face mask and ear plugs and especially using a dust extractor. Of course I followed John's lead. Less cautious though, I did without the mask and ear plugs.

John went on to complete a trout in two halves with fibre optic cable threaded through to the eyes. He had it mounted, a savagely dental piece of work on a kind of trolley which no one could fail to love except his wife who covered it with a white cloth.

Near the end of the year, I accompanied John to a meeting of the Utah Woodcarvers' Association ('March will be another whopper meeting' said the blurb), helping him to carry a dust extractor he'd invented which he claimed was almost silent when operating. First, he introduced me: 'John's a poet – he will read you a poem if you like'. Under peaked caps, rows of eyes voted no. Then John demonstrated his machine which promptly blew out the brains of the guys in the first rows. John was a generous friend. On my departure he gave me a piece of that old, trusted technology, a leather strop. I still use it.

In his inventiveness, his brazen creativity, John rivalled Kevin and Caradoc, encountered years before. I was in Prestatyn; they were from Llysfaen; they were fixing our roof and one of them ordered steel

The process of making a little ringed plover
Stage 1 – carving; Stage 2 – burning; Stage 3 – painting

Marilyn Davies

springs for what he called his 'kangaroo boots' in the interests of speed. Would the spring be better in the heel or the toe? And the other, a golfer, was experimenting with a mirror fixed to his putting club that offered a variety of angles showing the hole. Our roofing job lasted only three days. I wished it had been longer.

In the same year we were also invited to attend the Wasatch Whittlers' Club. It was all very competitive in an unapologetic way. 'Guys,' said the local expert, 'if you wanna compete at the highest level you got to improve your feathering, anatomy, beak technology and everything else.' We braced ourselves. Of course we wanted to compete. Vague memories of British clubs faded. Near the end of the evening a doctor who taught a first aid class in his spare time had a tale to tell. A student saw a child knocked down by a car and proceeded to use what he'd learned about splinting and bandaging. Later the doctor saw the results. 'Son,' he said to the proud class member, ' you've saved that boy's life.' Modest smile from the apprentice. 'Yep,' the doctor went on. 'If you'd put the splint on the leg that was broken you'd have killed him.'

* * *

It was a few years earlier, in 1983, that we had met Stan Taylor in the Tacoma Mall in Washington State. He sat on a chair, presiding over a table in a main 'street'. A retired businessman, he had given up shooting ducks for carving and painting them. A small bird took him up to thirty hours. It starts, he said, with a block of wood (basswood in America or lime in British terms) on which he draws top and side patterns. Cutting out on a bandsaw should take about twenty minutes. So what takes the rest of the time? Well, mainly whittling the bird with consideration for bilateral symmetry so you end up with a rounded bird. Stan waxed eloquent about the difficulties of that.

A patient, relaxed man, Taylor was a good teacher. Woodcarvers rarely hesitate to share their knowledge, divulging such secrets as the making of bird feet. I tend towards a simple approach with various grades of wire but Stan was more committed to realism, lead being soldered over the wired legs and details like toenails added with a knife. Stan emphasized that he didn't want his bird carving to become a business; he didn't want the pleasure principle to rust into work.

I envied Stan the boat which took him around Puget Sound or to islands off the coast in search of driftwood. But I did not envy him the notices around his house which said 'This room has been cleaned'. I bought a wren unpainted because I didn't share Stan's taste in colours. Neither do I trust mine. I don't paint my birds: someone else more skilful and patient does it. And that someone is my wife Marilyn who barbs and paints all my work. This is how she describes the process:

'Once John has finished the carving, it's usually over to me. The first stage is to use a pyrography tool to produce the texture of the feathers. Although this seems a tedious procedure, I enjoy it and find it a gentle way in to the actual painting. The machine has various pens or blades which can be heated to a range of temperatures. A low temperature will produce a light mark and hundreds of these barbs are required to give the bird a feathery look. At a high temperature, the tool can also be used to produce dark brown markings. Sometimes, with a bird such as a curlew, which is basically white and brown, white paint or dye and the use of pyrography is all that is required. Compared with a paintbrush, even a very fine one, it's more accurate. But most birds will be painted. Many British birds are what birders call 'little brown jobs', so achieving shades of brown and grey is vital. The colours I use most are earth tones: Raw Umber, Burnt Umber, Raw Sienna, Burnt Sienna, and White. I rarely use black as it is hardly ever found in nature, preferring Vandyke Brown or a mixture of Raw Umber and Payne's Grey or Burnt Umber and Ultramarine. Similarly, most whites need to be toned down. The paints I use are acrylics which being water-based can be diluted with water. I apply fairly thin washes so as not to lose the texture I've just been working on. Ideally, although the whole surface is covered, you should be able to sense the wood underneath and occasionally we'll use wood dyes instead of paint. But fortunately, for the sake of variety, there are some birds which allow a wider palette. The obvious example is the kingfisher. As well as the vivid colours, this requires a certain amount of iridescence

Marilyn in the workshop

John Davies

which is achieved by using iridescent powders or iridescent medium. This is also found on lapwings and some ducks. We've also enjoyed the outlandish colours of the red-legged partridge.'

Chapter 4: The Wards and Gilley

In September 1987, during a year in Utah, we visited the local woodworkers' club where we met Byron Cheever who invited us over to see his decoy collection. It turned out that Byron used to be the editor of the monthly **North American Decoys** and he'd written several books on the subject. 'Decoy' means, in Dutch, 'cage' or 'lure' and the idea was to entice flocks down to water level by the sight of relaxed 'birds' apparently feeding. They were anchored. Birds were an invaluable source of food and anybody was free to shoot over any marsh or river – as was not the case in Europe. I'd assumed that decoys were an American invention. But at Lovelock Cave in Nevada in 1924, archeologists discovered eleven well-preserved decoys dated at more than a thousand years old. Composed of reeds bound together in the shape of a floating bird, they were covered in a skin of the bird with feathers to add realism.

Byron had a gift for us. It was a book, written by him, richly illustrated, entitled **The Ward Brothers**, and even now it lights up my carving life. The Ward brothers, Lem (1897-1984) and Steve (1895-1976), revolutionized the art of carving painted ducks and geese. Born in the 1890s in Crisfield, on Chesapeake Bay, they were hunters from an early age. Barbers at first, as hunting grew more popular especially during the hungry nineteen-thirties, they spent more time on their decoys. In 1933 haircuts were fifteen cents and decoys sold for a dollar and twenty-five cents. Steve ('you have to live it') and Lem ('we didn't pattern after nobody') defined the terms of their success.

The average decoy was rough and ready. In the Chesapeake style, head positions were usually straight forward. There are examples of turned head decoys, but these were generally shunned as being impractical and hard to handle. Heads were fastened by nails driven down through the top of the head into the body. Far outnumbering the rest were the highly desirable canvasback ducks which came in great numbers to feed on the wild rice and celery beds of the Bay. Almost

Kingfisher

Peter Hughes

from the beginning the Wards' decoys were superior. And the local opposition kept copying their work so it got to the point where 'we would make three or four models until the competition got so disgusted they all quit trying'.

In terms of their development, an early experimental stage was followed by cedar birds displaying a level of realism not seen in other decoys of the period. Then came a simpler decoy with a balsa body and pine or cedar head; simpler paint patterns because of the increased rate of production; and Steve started to make miniature decoys. The 1960s saw Lem creating highly decorative birds often with elaborate displays of preening or wing-stretching, and also a wider variety of birds including grouse, shorebirds and a peregrine falcon. As Steve said at the time: Lem was never satisfied – not least in the flexibility of his response to the market. He was one of the first to introduce stippling (dots) to reduce shine and for decorative purposes. They won the big decoy competition in New York in 1948 and their broad-billed drake, made in 1936, was sold in 2013 for $51,750.

The most impressive Ward decoy I've seen was a Canada goose (1965) in which a quiet tidal movement of lines with growing space between laps the neck then spreads out as it approaches the tail, a subtle dark green. Simplicity rules harmony of all body lines. Writes Byron Cheever: 'Lem dips his brush and drips it on a glass to get the brush hairs straight and to a feathering point. Then he can make as many as seventy-five strokes before he has to fill it again.'

What explains the impact of the decoy? It has long ago drifted away from hunting. But it's a reminder of hunting, and of wide spaces capable of great variety. It's relatively small and shapely enough to win its place in the living room.

The slaughter of wildfowl eventually had its consequences. A number of species of duck became scarce, the Labrador duck became extinct. The last passenger pigeon died in 1916 in Cincinnati Zoo. Public concern resulted in Congress passing the Migratory Birds Act in 1918. It put an end to 'market hunting' which had flourished for nearly seventy years.

* * *

Wendell Gilley wasn't around when we called at Southwest Harbor, Maine, mainly to visit his museum. Like the Wards, Gilley went from shooting to recreating, their workaday lives (the Wards were barbers, Gilley was a plumber) transformed. By the 1970s, sometimes more than a hundred visitors a day flocked to the Gilley home. It must have cost considerable physical and commercial effort to establish the Wendell Gilley Museum, a lot of it due to his conviviality. He welcomed visitors to his studio, happy to share his knowledge as he worked. He also published a book, **The Art of Bird Carving** (1972), a characteristically patient, helpful volume that's had a long life. By his estimate, he created 'ten thousand birds of pine and paint'. Gilley loved alliteration; most of his carvings were made of basswood.

After our visit I was stirred to write a poem about one bird with such a commanding air that I suppressed a salute. The concluding lines are:

> It could have swept earth's contours
> through the air, beaten darkness senseless.
> Bird in the wood. Wood in the bird.
> Whichever way you looked at it,
> his barn owl, you were looking up.
> 'At Southwest Harbor'

Gilley's work lives on. The last I heard, the museum had three full-time employees including a full-time woodcarver and arranges a range of exhibitions.

Chapter 5: From the river
(Excerpts from letters sent by John Davies)

Met a fellow down by the river this week. I hadn't seen him for a year since he announced himself as a photographer/painter, recently retired from the Army. Apparently he spent hundreds of pounds on an exhibition at Rhyl library where Hope goes to die. And his expensive camera was damaged and he was harassing (he couldn't afford to sue) the insurers... I was reminded of you. Except he is mad. He claimed that he was superb at languages, offering as evidence someone who'd addressed him in Greek to which he'd responded in English – and was **understood**. He speaks languages, it seems, telepathetically. Then he did say something reminiscent of you: he was going to Dallas where there's a woman who 'thinks the world of me'. And he thinks speaking Welsh will be useful there.

* * *

I felt the faint stirrings of creative writing myself (but nothing will come of it) a fortnight ago. I was down by the river where I'd seen the occasional seal, disguised as a football rolling on the tide. This time, I found one dead, furry and young; attached to its tail was the tag 'London Zoo'. It's a crime story. Somcone selling off animals and ... But there my imagination gives up.

* * *

I met a genuine Woodman last week, near Ysceifiog, after a tip-off. Lurking in an immobile home near a long metal shed and some woodland he owns, he emerged with sawdust in his hair, ears and croaky voice, the last of his kind. He was purporting to sell wood but was more interested in simply shed-dwelling. It's the only volcanic shed I've ever seen, spouting soft brown ash that has fossilised his tools and dust-thumped flowers on the spiders' webs in his one small window. To shuffle across his deeply-layered floor is to experience an archeological dig. He has disappeared so far into his work that if he stood out in the woodland he'd be a dust storm, a sculpture in rain.

* * *

I was walking by the river this week when I met a member of one of my ex-evening classes. 'What are you doing?' she asked. I rhapsodised about a lump of wood I'd hidden earlier, apparently a worthless green lump that, when I turned it over, became a gift from the great god Craft. 'Going to burn it are you?' she asked.

* * *

Like members of a nomadic tribe (some have tents), we craftspeople of the north east of Wales keep meeting and disbanding at a variety of shows and fairs through the summer months. We're chasing the buffalo. Which are often hard to find. They certainly weren't at the Great Eccleston Show for which I'd paid under the impression that this was the Eccleston near Chester, an error I had plenty of time to regret during four journeys along the M6 to and from Lancaster. The buffalo were, however, at the St Asaph Woodfest, grazing contentedly with their fat wallets bulging, and they were to be found too at the Cheshire Show where our tribe had gathered as The Welsh Village, a compound of caterers, craftspeople and tourist agencies under the red dragon. I do hope the buffalo will be at the Shrewsbury Flower Show because I've paid £250 for shooting rights.

* * *

Another filmic scene was provided by the members of the Pensychnant Nature Trust whom I addressed recently. A founder member left them his mansion years ago, filled with stuffed birds, and

John in the workshop

Marilyn Davies

it's a cosy venue on a bleak November afternoon when the fires are lit. It's a decaying venue though and the long drive up to it keeps subsiding forgetfully. The conservatory had trapped a feeble yellow light which sat in two deckchairs contemplating the kind of lawnmower with which Panama hats used to be given free. In that remote spot, at that misty time, the twenty or so members seemed like survivors of some cult, ghosting out of the undergrowth to ask if Maggie Thatcher was still prime minister.

* * *

Yesterday I was at Conwy RSPB as part of a two-day demonstration. On being told at the desk that we have a woodcarver with us today, demonstrating his craft, one dry Lancastrian eyed me as I flicked my knife at a plover half-heartedly and asked, 'When's he starting?' One fellow described movingly how he'd been stranded after retirement from a local factory. He'd started dreaming of the lads at work and becoming depressed. Then he found love spoons. He was still depressed I think, but too busy to notice.

* * *

The characteristic movement in north Wales is that of the farming Welsh, weary after years of thankless labour, passing on their way downhill the urban English, tired of city life, on their eager way up towards seclusion, peace. I met members of the new order recently, Miles and Pip, who'd bought a dishevelled farmhouse at the end of a troubled lane on a hillside near Corwen. They plan to turn the place into a spiritual retreat.

* * *

The highlight, on the last day, was the sound of martial drumming in the park and we discovered twenty kids, led by their teacher, who'd been trained in precision drumming, But what made it unforgettable was that they used plastic bottles which they beat on the rim of the municipal fountain. It's the art that touches me most. It's the Ward brothers who were barbers and hunters and turned into decoy carvers of the highest order. It's Peter Prendergast who lived among slate quarries in north Wales and used the most unscenic of scenery for art because that was home. Something with the primitive in it.

* * *

I was by the river yesterday when an acquaintance hailed me from the walkway above. He was with a band of about fifteen Welsh speakers whom he identified as members of the Edward Llwyd Society. And now he addressed them on my behalf, a few words like 'Marilyn Davies' and 'Y Glannau' (the local Welsh newspaper) standing out from the blizzard. He paused. His enthusiastic followers gazed down at me expectantly. All I could do was address them in the wrong language. The pain lodged itself with various other key moments in my life, not least that moment at Brigham Young University when I pretended to speak Welsh and was found out by ... No, no, it's too painful still.

* * *

In my visit to a primary school in Abergele, seventy children were doing a project on trees and I was to talk about wood. My teaching style, I quickly realised, is characterised by a lot of rhetorical questions so when I declaimed, 'Early on, of course, the question was: where was I going to find wood to carve?' a thicket of arms shot up and at the base of one a mouth opened and declared, 'From trees'. Later their questions left me drained, newly impressed by the resilience and resource of primary school teachers.

* * *

I had a note from Kyffin Williams last week asking if I'd say a few words about his new exhibition for the S4C programme Heno. Assuming that I'd been chosen because I **look** Welsh, I practised Celtic gestures and dark looks in the mirror but then I learned that, after all, a Welsh-speaker was required.

* * *

Recently, I visited Hay-on-Wye, a town struggling to get free of its inland sea of books, it seems to me. The shopfronts look undisturbed but stiff tides of paper slump into basements, lap shelves and swell into attics. Visitors keep trying to bale out the town but make little headway. My contribution was to remove a gorgeous book of paintings by the nineteenth-century bird artist, John Gould. Later we visited Kilvert's house in Clyro because I read his diaries at regular intervals, much liking that calm, sane voice. Apparently he kept his diaries because 'life appears to me such a curious and wonderful thing that it seems almost a pity that even such a humble and uneventful life as mine should pass altogether away without some record as this, and partly too because I think the record may amuse and interest some who come after me'. Which seems a welcome alternative to the oft-touted reason for writing: the transmission of greatness.

Chapter 6: Holmes and wood thoughts

In 1970 when Clyde Holmes moved with his German wife Gudrun from London to a rented cottage about five hundred feet above Bala, Cwm Hesgin, it wasn't all plain sailing. They had no car, no running water, no electricity. Neighbouring farmers helped with items of furniture. And the local shepherd used to watch them from the hillside, bloody hippies. But the Holmeses persevered. They installed a propane gas stove, a hand-operated washing machine and a battery-operated transistor radio. By 1992 water had been diverted in a quarter-mile leat from a headspring to a point near the house where a water wheel would generate electricity.

People started coming. I visited half a dozen times during the early nineties, liking the family, their tenuous hold on the previous century, the way their dog sat on the track facing back to the house because he couldn't bear seeing people (especially the Holmeses) leave. The Holmes family were outlasting the farmers who, twenty years previously, had predicted their imminent departure.

Gudrun worked on translations then later at a gift shop in Bala. The owner, an Englishman, refused to employ the average locals. And the couple grew to a family of five, the pleasures of the outdoor life including a small lake with a boat, nesting marsh harriers and snowdrifts.I knew Bjorn best, a pupil at Ysgol y Berwyn where, I was intrigued to hear, the farm boys were known as 'joskins'. One night, leaving, I glanced back at the cottage seemingly embedded in the hill under one cone of light.

Back in 1970 Clyde had been looking for a place where he could develop his art. The barn next to the cottage was it, cold but serviceable. Clyde had trained in the early sixties. Now he painted their high valley over and over as if determined to get it right. He was aiming at a fusion of land, light and cloud shadow, the changing face of the landscape. 'In my painting I've been attempting to express the silent dialogue between light and dark.' At best he'd produce epic

Firecrests

Marilyn Davies

imagery; at worst he would not have opened a dialogue at all. The landscape as a place of history didn't seem to interest him. If he knew of the political implications of the name Llyn Celyn (which his smallholding virtually overlooked) or of Camp Frongoch (where IRA prisoners faced bleak years and heard, to their surprise, their guards conversing in Welsh), I don't know. But anyway there would have been much else to consider. The Holmeses had to stop milking their goats and growing their own vegetables when radiation levels shot up after the Chernobyl cloud passed over, affecting them more intensely than anywhere else in the area. And then there were the low-flying fighter jets on manoeuvres from the RAF Valley base in Anglesey, shattering the silence.

His paintings are large, mountains bristling with reeds churned up by clouds. His work was shown in an Artists in National Parks exhibition which toured the country, then the United States. The titles are archetypal: Light Pool, Torn Shadow, Rush Lightfall, River Wall. Said Clyde, 'I used to name my paintings after places but now I use different titles. It liberates them and makes them more universal.' It is the style of the times, an honest view. But how much is lost if a landscape is named Anywhere?

Then again, Cwm Hesgin stood in what Clyde described as 'wilderness'. But it had been a spiritual centre, a peat-gathering centre, a sheep-shearing centre. 'Empty' space is a debating chamber into which, for instance, stepped the novelist C.P. Snow to challenge the American poet Robert Frost:

'Then he spoke about what he called 'the locative' in art. Art which meant anything to him was locative, rooted in a place, in the singularities of a place. We had a bit of an argument. Temperamentally, I said, I was on his side. But locative art needs knowledge and patience to understand: that was why cosmopolitan art, abstract art, travelled farther and faster. One didn't have to know anything to read, say, Kafka or Hemingway. They had travelled around the world to an extent that Jane Austen or Forster never would. Frost wouldn't have it. The greatest locative art transcended everything, it was organic and no other art could be.'

(C.P. Snow on Robert Frost)

Clyde's poems, unlike his paintings, are small, detailed, closing in on birds, animals, plants: locative art. He painted only in natural light. In the evenings he worked on his poetry lit by paraffin lamps and candles. In 1997 Clyde was featured on television in the documentary series **Visions of Snowdonia** (BBC), narrated by Anthony Hopkins. He shaped his own life against the odds and left me awestruck in the process. He died in 2008, aged 67.

Seagulls

Above cliffs
clouds drift with them.

Sun, a dazzling brooch
on their staggering breasts.

Wings make shadows on them,
fly in waterfalls of light.

Bodies of sea
wings of sky.

Owl

Sits alone
in the sycamore.
His moaning coos
waver through darkness,
our window-glare
his night's oasis.

We move around
in the house, project
our brief shadows.
He echoes life's eclipses,
our pining for light.

Chickens

Are senseless in the dark -

reborn every morning
with the cock's bugling.

Deep-pink glow of combs
   sunrise their heads
   sparring with shed's
   rectangle of fresh light.

   Inveterate scratchers -
   claw-roots in soil.
   All day beaks peg ground.

   Fold themselves up
   before night comes -

   always ahead of the sun.

* * *

The hunt for wood teaches you. At Powis Castle sawmill I faced a group of workers lunching in a Portakabin. 'Any decent hardwood?' They stared. 'Any dry hardwood?' One was moved to confession: '-ish'. And what is the moral of this tale? Follow through. I lacked follow-through. Or take the beach at Llanddulas where an old man, years back, said he'd seen a nice lump of mahogany but his wife wouldn't have it in the car. By the time he'd returned home to Bodelwyddan then sneaked back, the wood had gone. The moral is clear: marry careful.

There are many good days in the quest for wood. I think of random successes. There was that bank of the Clwyd: on its edge above the water, a head of intertwined bare branches. It was beautiful. But surely it was too good? Someone planted it there? No. Take it and run. And the first day of my retirement, walking with Clyde to Llyn Hesgin with a young buzzard calling, circling as we ate my sandwich. He had a new painting, new poems. I had a new start.

The older I've become, the more that wood collecting seems the most attractive part of the business. Certainly I don't start with a bird. I start with a river-given perch and increasingly I make my own perches from collections of twigs screwed together. Nothing can beat sun striking matches on the water, birds blown and the lighthouse peering over the dunes. I read in my notes of years ago: 'carried on with my eight curlew sandpipers' (2001); I'm astonished. I wouldn't do that now: two is enough.

Beware friends bearing gifts: drying wood isn't an exact science and central heating is its enemy.

The staple question at the stands in craft fairs is: 'How long does it take?' One craftsman in Shrewsbury wore a T-shirt which answered **Bloody Ages**. To be more specific as regards time and cost, these factors need to be considered:

Little stint

Chris Porteous

- How hard is the wood?
- Carving feathers is a slow business.
- Feathers with barbs burned by pyrography, doubly so.
- A turned (90°) head involves more time than a straight-on look, but both can be managed with a bandsaw.
- Any other angle and using the bandsaw becomes tricky.
- Adding open wings should cost at least twice the standard model.

Carving a pair of realistic legs is ... But fear not, the desperate look in your craftsman's eye means that he, at least, will be realistic in terms of price.

Chapter 7: Algieri

'One winter's evening, crouching in a gutter, hidden in the reeds I was searching the sky for flighting mallard. Then I see three approaching, their flight path straight over me and well in range. I'm concentrating, keeping very still. To my astonishment I notice a peregrine falcon flying at right angles from the nearby cliff and my eyes are transfixed. It flies like an exocet missile down towards the flighting mallard – surely it will take one out? But, at the last second, the mallard must have seen the peregrine and folded its wings, plummeting like a stone. The peregrine hurtles past unable to change course.'

That's an entry from the journal of Pierino Algieri (1955 -), a retired conservation officer and photographer who wrote **Pierino's Snowdonia** (Gwasg Carreg Gwlach, 2013). Those two occupations proved complementary: Pierino has a detailed knowledge of his home area of Llanddoged in the Conwy Valley. He has exhibited in galleries and lectured to many photography groups. If you want to know the sound of a buzzard diving onto a plastic decoy or learn how a cormorant operates underwater in a large pool when you're parked in the tree above it or, if you need as a bird carver, really good driftwood for perches... Pierino's your man.

We have known each other for almost twenty years. We first met at a craft fair, me with my stall of painted, wooden birds, him with his photography. They were all-day affairs, sunny surprisingly often, in which conversational fragments from the passing crowd could relieve a dull day:

'How's you on-goingness?'

'If anyone comes in skinny and goes out fat, I'll know about it.'

'Reading his wife's diary is one thing. Correcting her spelling is another.'

On one of our first walks along the Conwy from Betws-y-Coed, I felt more sharply observant, spotting sand martin nests in holes in the

Dunlin

Keith Millward

banks. But then he saw a dipper's nest under a bridge, and a splash of Himalayan balsam. And a cormorant on the shingle. Not moving, said Pierino, because he's young or over-fed.

Pierino told me the story of his brother-in-law in the Cwm Eidda valley. He noticed pied wagtails following his Massey Ferguson tractor and then, a few days later, he opened the bonnet. He was amazed to find a pied wagtail nest on the engine block, which contained three chicks; and they all fledged safely. I was heartened by this, the survival of the seemingly fragile creatures in the face of the roaring machine. The only poem about a tractor that I know is this wonder by R S Thomas (from 'Cynddylan on a tractor'):

> Riding to work now as a great man should,
> He is the knight at arms breaking the fields'
> Mirror of silence, emptying the wood
> Of foxes and squirrels and bright jays.
> The sun comes over the tall trees
> Kindling all the hedges, but not for him
> Who runs his engine on a different fuel.
> And all the birds are singing, bills wide in vain,
> As Cynddylan passes proudly up the lane.

How skilful is the merging of two virtual opposites: mock admiration and bitter lament for the same man and the countryside. The roaring of the tractor is just as loud as in the story told by Pierino. But whereas the pied wagtails didn't seem bothered by it, Cynddylan is seen as its victim – destroying silence, driving birds and animals away. And the poem ends in false majesty with a rhyming couplet that emphasizes how Cynddylan is deceived. Whatever happens to you matters less than how you respond to it.

How did this Welsh-speaker, born in Trefriw, become Pierino Algieri? Well, his father Vincenzo was captured at Tobruk in 1943, then transferred to a high security POW camp at Llanrwst. The soldiers were made to wear red patches on their uniforms identifying them as fascists. In time many of them worked on farms in the local area and

Vincenzo ended up at Llanddoged – where Pierino lives today. It's also the village in which Vincenzo's future wife lived. Elizabeth (Betty)'s mother was raised in Liverpool but her family fell on misfortune and she was sent to Wales as a lady's companion. Betty's father did not look kindly on this relationship so she and Vincenzo eloped, returning when the dust had settled. Eventually they took over a farm near Maenan and raised a big family. Betty is still alive.

Pierino inherited countrymen's skills from his father. In particular those involved in putting food on the table such as shooting pigeons; Pierino still uses the family recipe. They were a self-sufficient family, rearing turkeys, geese and pigs. Rereading **Pierino's Snowdonia** I was struck – technical matters aside because they're beyond me – by the human qualities the craft of photography requires. A strong visual awareness is not a gift given to everyone. Knowledge is also welcome, better when garnished with chopped-up information. Take this comment – he says of wild garlic: 'I often crush the flowers or leaves, enjoying the garlic aroma. I have used the flowers as a cooking ingredient when making pasta sauce'. Or, in his commentary on Llyn Geirionydd, Pierino says: 'The waters are quite acidic, from old mines. There are some small brown trout to be found at the northern end'. The precisely detailed voice is recognisably that of the fish conservancy officer. Knowledge and appreciation of cooking will have come at least partly from his Italian father. Some knowledge is intuitive: 'I often avoid sheep in my pictures as their white colour can be distracting to the eye, but for this picture they really work as their staggered line breaks up the repetitive middle ground'. If not knowledge, at least trust in one's taste can stimulate: 'I found the white-washed walls were too stark and lacked emotion'.

As well as knowledge, enthusiasm lights up Pierino's commentary. Whether freezing in bad weather or rising for a dawn which doesn't yield light ('Light! Light!'), he is patient. Or at least tolerant: 'Unfortunately Menai Bridge is partly hidden but you can't have it all your own way all of the time'. Then another hard-won rumination comes along or an interesting fact: 'My great great grandfather, David William Evans, was the manager of Rhos quarry in Capel Curig during

Curlew sandpiper

Marilyn Davies

the period 1860 – 1900'. And he has such energy ... Best take breaks. The photographs are brilliant.

I've often heard Pierino describe the joys of fishing at Llyn Conwy. The new season is eagerly awaited in a lonely place where solitude, though, is not always available. Red kites, hen harriers, merlin – not to mention the great black-backed gulls which nest on an island in the lake – will dive bomb you screaming and squawking if you venture too near their nests. Their large wingspan and vicious-looking beaks could inflict serious injuries and he has often considered wearing a protective hat. With this warning, I leave you hatless to face alone a merlin attack from Pierino's journal:

'On a bright, crisp winter's day after a very hard frost I was wandering around Llyn Lockwood near Pen y Gwryd taking photographs of Snowdon. I noticed a hawk (which I'm almost certain was a merlin) chasing a snipe near the lake. The snipe suddenly dived into the tall rushes only to be followed by the relentless merlin. I saw the limp body of the snipe being carried in the merlin's talons where it landed on a fence post and proceeded to tear and devour the little bird. I left it alone, watching through my binoculars, plumes of snipe feathers floating in the breeze. When the merlin flew off I went over to investigate the kill. The only evidence I could see apart from feathers was the snipe's beak and skull which looked like a skewer left on top of the post.'

Chapter 8: Poetry by John Davies

Charles Tunnicliffe

The last white of day is brushed through dark
blues into magpie almost not there.
Tunnicliffe painted it. This late, still in place.
Seeking exactness, he found art, let facts suggest
what could translate given time, shape, space,
into the ungiven that never rests.

The next page flutters. And, a whole clifftop
in its grip, his hawk with wings half-spread
is about to launch it. What seem models of restraint,
They were reference points with which paint
made free, of which a floating brush made light.

His mallards do with dignity what ducks do best,
upend it. Curlew like seaweed in the rain,
clumps of a khaki shore, await sky's outcome.
Such making stirs ours. Details inform the mind
so art can teach (fingers flex and drum) –
up to the point where art leaves information behind.

Wings

Time hadn't mattered till her husband's ran out.
The house, spreading, made an evening of itself.
Reedy flats stretching out to a horse
and banging door for company met roofs on the run
from dunes. Careful, afternoons measured
the estuary where tides weighed logs
then put them down, where hours drowned like clouds.

When the ex-minister, fifties like her, kept calling,
his beard through pipe-smoke she read first
as contentment. He had seen the world and shrugged.
Wrong, he had dabbled in property till it bit him.
He'd collect firewood, taking logs for a stroll
in a stripped pram, put up coveys of gull
brought down as he tracked the shoreline. She saw
not washed-up footprints, water quicken slippery
as wind past the lighthouse, rippling implications.
Ships had been juggled long distance till its arms shrank.

The roof leaked. Mornings he'd spread planks, tools
and disappear. He'd finished the process
of getting started. And would have finished
the job but then the roofing season ended.

Once at dusk when she'd thrown stale bread,
the window floating, floating with white wings
settled on water. Not just perspective though
of the opposite shore kept sea dreams in check.
He wanted to preach again so she fixed up
practices at Seion, listened from the empty pews
and drove him home. Theirs was an oldish house.
The roof seemed shaky but faith might hold it up.

View from the Workshed

I

Quick. A squirrel
launching the glider of its tail
flies up a trunk.

I watch what my hands
make of bandsawn wood.
Not much usually
though hands don't know that,
and anyway even our apple tree
flares only once a year.
Twisting, it can't untie its knot.

But it gives rise to birds, give rise.
Carved birds too want to live,
blocked wings become wing blur,
heads turn to their shadows.
How to grasp what flies?

Catch, say, the dark star trilling
before it is a skylark.

The workshop

Keith Millward

II

And another
I can't catch:
the raven of Moel Ddu
in its own sky,

that watches a path run
straight to the quarry.
Again it circles
the chapel's torn covers.

It will not follow
where streams weary
of light-splitting
idle their last laps.

It keeps, bearded, high
places. It ministers
to a quarry, lake,
a chapel that once

glimpsed souls fly up
so perfectly healed
no scars were visible.
And won't sink lower.

IV

Lots of ways, yes,
of getting it wrong.

Say early on
you lost proportion.

Or flaws you can't
smooth out join up.

Live into it:
things made from scratch

and scowl don't work.
How well you do

still counts when
it's what you have to do.

Symmetry's hard late on,
you get lopsided.

Overall,
carving's easier.

Ray's Birds

Lunchtime, the way he tells it,
with Ray weightless, orbiting
the forgotten planet Stress,
his chickens screech SOS
so he's off. Fox?
No, they're spun shuttlecocks
because just yards away
stands a peregrine on a jay
quivering, spread to take the spike.
Ray drifts dreamlike.
When the falcon lifts and its full load
drags it down, he lunges, rolls
to save the jay, jaycrazy,
grabs a leg. And sits up. Dazed,
he's got the falcon. Flared eyes
flash beak. Ray makes – crabwise
past the pigeon loft, on wings --
for his shed, shuffles in, gets string,
gets stabbed, ties one leg to a brick towed
clattering. Leaps out. Shed explodes.

"So what now, Ray?" That's Rosalie,
unacquainted with falconry.
His arm with clenched fist
lifts. Air swoops, glory clamps his wrist
"What'll it eat?" is Ray's sole doubt,
who spends days not finding out
then tries pigeon, desperate. It's his.
For the peregrine another bloody quiz.
Chasing its eyes around, it picks
at the soft corpse, flicking

to feather it. And pecks. And tears
raw treasure – soon, compère
of the feast, Ray's killed another three.
His top racing birds look queasy.
The falcon hops on his leather glove
to stare, his lethal turtle-dove.

Rosalie sums up, unflinching
the whole strange thing:
"You've got to let it go".
The sky's big through that shed window,
Ray has had doubts. It's young,
so demandingly high-strung
he has no time to live in.
And he's running out of pigeon.
So he pulls the door, stands
back. Loud hoovering woodland,
an astonishment of light,
yank the fat bird right
through the cramped frame
of all that's tame
in the world of walls
out to a radiant, rayless windfall.

But Ray has wings still. Weeks later,
watching his fastest bird home straight
towards Bishop's Wood,
he'd fly too if he could.
End of a race. His timer's ready, best
time, the loft a home-made nest.
Ray's eyes
are full of sky.
Then, higher, he sees it, black
cross, black skyjack.
That falcon, tapping its wings on air
plummets, hits four-square
his pigeon gone south
before Ray can close his mouth.
And a puff of brown
feathers filters down.
Ray's there like a praying mantis.
Don't tell him I told you this.

Decoys

This poem is meant as a dialogue between me and Harold Gill.

My timber for carving's from the shore,
driftlumps water sluices out
so it dries fast and won't crack. Elm most of all.
Bones in the woodshed's drought,
they clench. Opened months later, a store
of ripeness surprised is the windfall.

We'd leave for Mostyn, cross
the Shrouds. You had to know the water.
What use is a duck-punt once a week?
You're not informed. Birds on the ebb won't stir,
just sit there packed. The flood brings chaos.
High tide meant hide-and-seek.

I carve birds, ducks often: pintail
and mallard, a teal, shapes wood lays for the hand.
Bandsaw for roughing out – check the grain
runs with the bill. Chisels, rasp. Elm is hard sand.
With oil or polish, what's been fingered stale,
another late surprise, is sunburnt terrain.

Each day – start early. We liked NE
in the face when we picked our spot:
no wobblings, steady as she ... Sixty yards
for a clean kill. 20 ounces. AA shot.
But for food, I wouldn't have killed – at least
not birds. Smooth the feathers, keep no scorecard.

    Best I like the curve where crown, cheek,
    sweep down through the swell of chest,
    the sweptback, cleared-for-action prow
    of a poised gathering unrest
    that, from the moment's peak,
    through wood, might just take off, go anyhow.

Sources

Sometime I'd like to go to Crisfield, Maryland,
where "two dumb old country boys" with a barber's shop
saved themselves for other business to hand:
carved birds, imagination's airdrop

out of cleared skies. All they borrowed from was memory.
Their decoys' upswept bills, cocked heads, are records
of how life drawn to art takes off again, how teals,
canvasbacks and pintails become Wards.

Would I find things changed there on Chesapeake Bay?
You bet. What beckons though like a country road:
the illusion that where men lived is halfway
to how they saw. Which can be borrowed.

West in poet Hugo's steps years back, I tried placing
him at the Skagit, as if that darkly running song,
his secret, still floated. Cold water. Why trace
the source when a river is so long?

He'd left Port Townsend too. It was a waterspout,
flung acres of ferries everywhere, sending -
with drops at Bremerton, Seattle – right out
to the Pacific then infinity the town's end.

To locate is to limit glittering lines of contact.
Best open yourself, not haunt abandoned yards.
Still, words are not wood. His poem "The Swimmer at ..."
Sometime I'd like to see Lake Edward.

Sedge warblers

Marilyn Davies

Chapter 9: Slate carvings, Rice and Thompson

In 1983 an exhibition launched at Bangor intrigued me: 'Llechi Cerfiedig Dyffryn Ogwen' (The Carved Slates of Dyffryn Ogwen). Could slate be carved? I turned up at Bangor – and, yes, of course there are slate tombstones, lettered. But these carvings were more ambitious. A pattern of circles on one of them encloses a representation of the Menai Suspension Bridge not long after it was built. Another slab has four diamond shapes containing plants probably representing the four seasons. A third slate is thought to have been made by John Parry, singer and composer of the tune **Friendship** who had it put up over his fireplace. The fireplace is a favourite site for these carvings which date from between 1823 and 1843, a period coinciding with the trebling of the workforce at Penrhyn Quarry. Probably the most impressive and largest (23½" x 14") carvings are the three astronomical diagrams from Bryn Twrw, Tregarth. They are carved in minute and perfect detail incorporating the comparative sizes of the planets and their orbits, along with explanations of eclipses and comets. These complex explanations are in Welsh.

From accounts given by local people it is clear that many such slates have been destroyed or disfigured. Apparently there is a strange reluctance to appreciate them even now, and a typical local reaction is that 'they were just made by ordinary men' or 'only local people carved them'. While it is hard to imagine most slates sitting comfortably in a modern living room, they have a place as folk art. Mostly anonymous, the men worked hard in dangerous conditions for twelve hours a day, walked two or three miles to work and back, tended their smallholdings and animals and carved items to adorn their homes. They invented the necessary tools, developed their own style and produced work of originality in a new medium.

The most impressive artefact in slate that I have seen was the slate bust of Gwilym Hiraethog (Dr William Rees, 1802-1883). It was a round face with a crisp beard tracing its outline, a face of Easter Island strength with a strong nose and eyebrow ridges. It was a face that deserved a better place than it had been given in Penrhyn Castle.

* * *

It was in the early nineties that I knew Billy Rice. He was about in his fifties, a bachelor, a Welsh-speaking builder off and on, unemployed in Blaenau Ffestiniog. I saw a handsome bowl of his at Bodelwyddan Castle – Billy had developed a unique method of turning slate by smoothing the outsides of bowls as well as the insides. His grandfather had helped, an engineer-fitter in the Votty slate mine. When I approached him, suspicious of his invention being stolen, I had to produce the name of a trusted Blaenau man before he agreed to my visit.

Now he had his own workshop, a quiet man with a white beard and a foxy grin. He had worked at David Nash's place. He got his own shine for the slate, a special formula not the usual linseed oil and he liked Bethesda's slate best, its range of colours. This was a time of flux for him. He'd been to a craft fair at Newtown where a representative from Disney World expressed an interest in buying items for gift shops there. He had had a small order from the Garden Festival at Ebbw Vale. He was torn between such offers and the time-consuming one-offs such as those exhibited at Bodelwyddan. Among them was a superb jellyfish. Reluctantly, he explained: the jellyfish comprised a bowl of Bethesda slate, green like compacted moss and a hanging skirt of rough slate. Was it a trick or was it art? Billy didn't know despite (or because of) my protestations on the side of art. He had not been to art college as I hadn't, and I knew the unease that gnawed at him.

* * *

Mary E Thompson was born in 1896 of parents with independent means and extensive gardens in Devon. But she did her best work in north Wales quarries. She studied landscape painting under the noted Belgian artist Emile Fabry at St Ives and then spent three years in

Treecreepers in sycamore

Peter Hughes

Brussels, at the Academy. Finding no opening in London, her eye turned to Gwynedd as a subject. Landscape occupied her until the mountain slopes were taken over by the Army in 1939. And then she made the vital decision and talked to the manager at the Penrhyn quarry. She would make her mark, producing pencil drawings of the quarrymen and their landscapes.

The men were 'tough on themselves but kind to me'. That she learned Welsh was a real asset as was her determination to draw tools and machinery exactly. She also learned to use the ladders to reach the lower galleries. 'To get a reasonably long day means getting up at 5 a.m., catching the 8 o'clock bus then climbing 1500 feet by a steep stony path.' And this despite being a dwarf with severe curvature of the spine.

Her slate drawings are full of information and, surprisingly, individual personalities. She died in 1981 and I wrote these lines during the 1990s, an excerpt from 'Riders, Walkers' (**Dirt Roads**, Seren, 1997):

> They had their place in the picture, cold, damp,
> for Mary E. Thompson at this time. Cramped
> by ill-health, she leant ambition's ladder up as far
> as the Brussels Academy but surfaced in Bethesda.
> From a split block, a small cloud of dust
> escapes; a pencil can feel rock's upthrust.
> She walked, climbed, and for almost twenty
> years the galleries she toured were quarried,
> sheet after sheet, as pale drawn workday
> faces against stone in all the colours of grey
> defied mass. In time, she could tell them who,
> when asked, pointing, "Pwy 'di'r un acw?"*

Who's that one there?

Mary E Thompson, college-educated, had few doubts. But she was a committed Christian. She didn't rest easy in the Age of Picasso and she rejected 'abstraction and abnormality which I feel to be a dead end'. In her sister's words, 'She saw nothing in abstracts'. Neither Rice nor Thompson lived in the world of high art, true, but their art was true not low. And they faced questions that would trouble major artists of the time.

A group of shorebirds

Marilyn Davies

Chapter 10: R S Thomas

R.S. Thomas has commented that, as an age-old way of life in the Welsh hills began to wither, 'I turned to birds'. His absorption in bird life, however, had been constant since his childhood in Holyhead when 'the pale, china-like eggs lying in the mud's cup' fascinated him. In 1954 birds led him from Manafon to Eglwysfach and the Dyfi salt marshes. He had applied for the benefice at the suggestion of his friend, the naturalist William Condry and the two of them later helped to establish Ynyshir Nature Reserve. Here were species 'there had been no hope of seeing in Manafon'. Thirteen years later came the move to Aberdaron, with the sea visible half a mile from the poet's window, and herring gulls calling. He loved the feeling of being right at the end of the peninsula where he could watch the sea birds migrating in spring and autumn. Further afield, he travelled abroad frequently on bird-watching trips, to Poland and Greece for instance.

As a poet and priest, he wrestled with ideas of the deity, finding Nature and the intellect at odds, his inclination often towards the former. Books, he says in 'Those Others', 'tell of the war/Of heart with head, leaving/The wild birds to sing/The best songs.' The natural world often provides an escape from mental agonising: he might 'listen instead to the wind's text/Blown through the roof, or the thrush's song' ('The Minister'). There is conflict between the beauty of bird song and the darker realities of life: 'the sharp tooth tearing its prey,/While a bird sang from a tall tree'. His is a restless intellect and he can never be content with the comforts of nature. In 'A Thicket in Lleyn', he says 'between two truths/there is only the mind to fly with'. This mind is constantly questioning:

> Who to believe?
> The linnet sings bell-like,
> a tinkling music. It says life
> is contained here: is a jewel

in a shell casket, lying
among down. There is another
voice, far out in space,
whose persuasiveness is the distance

from which it speaks.
> ('Voices')

The mind is always 'divided' between the here and now and the eternal. The duality is not straightforward. Although the bird's song sounds pretty, Thomas's choice of images is complicated. A 'bell-like' voice is pure, but the bell also tolls to announce a death. 'Tinkling' suggests a cheap sound lacking in complexity. And a casket, especially a lined one, could make one think of a coffin. The prettiness is ephemeral. The other voice has more gravitas, reflected in the long sentence that describes it. The poem ends on a question: there is no resolution, but the reader is taken on an interesting flight.

The mind's flights can seem untrustworthy: to fly, to think is to be at risk. 'Is there a far side/to an abyss, and can our wings/take us there?' he asks in 'Strands'. But risks must be taken. Struggle is all, the nature of life itself – especially the struggle with self. The setting of 'The Untamed' is his wife's garden, enclosed, civilised, where

> the silence
> Holds with its gloved hand
> The wild hawk of the mind.

> But not for long, windows,
>   Opening in the trees
> Call the mind back
>   To its true eyrie; I stoop
>   Here only in play.

Fieldfare

Peter Hughes

The gloved hand suggests both gardening and falconry. The mind must fly free, poetry resist 'the silence', and the pun on 'stoop' evokes mock absorption in the flowers while connecting the poet with a hawk that stoops on its prey. His bird imagery, however, reveals Thomas's identification with the hawk to be by no means characteristic. Predator birds become increasingly rare in his work. The masculine principle is less assertive than might have been supposed, 'the soft influence/Of birds' ('Valediction'), as in a garden, catching his imagination far more often than 'the inhuman cry/Of buzzards' ('The Minister'). Few men in the poems are graced with bird metaphors. By contrast, the delicacy of ballerinas, 'birds in taffeta' with their 'precise fluttering' ('Degas, The Dancing Class'), the gentleness of a girl who is 'a shy bird in the nest' ('The Evacuee'), the woman whose 'voice was the birds' envy' ('Perspectives') are praised in poems not specifically about women. Women's gentleness and generosity haunt his poems. 'The Way Of It' and 'A Marriage' are both tributes to the poet's wife, both bird songs, the latter an elegy for one 'who in life/had done everything/with a bird's grace'. In contrast, grinding into action, Cynddylan empties 'the wood/Of foxes and squirrels and bright jays' ('Cynddylan on a Tractor'). In 'The Minister', one of Morgan's few happy memories is of the girl who one day pressed an egg into his hand.

Little wonder that the workings of this 'divided mind' are expressed so often by birds, belonging at once to earth and the heavens, full of restless movement and a grace they tempt us to try to attain. Or that they should express a vital element in division, the flickering alertness of Thomas's quest for God and his awareness of conflict between nature's benevolence and its uncaring remoteness . In many poems birds express divine benevolence as in 'a message from God/delivered by a bird at my window, offering friendship' ('The Message'). On the other hand, an owl's can be 'the voice/of God in the darkness cursing himself/fiercely for his lack of love' ('Barn Owl').

In his later work, Thomas examines faith and doubt. In 'Sea-watching' he talks of faith or understanding as 'a rare bird':

> Ah, but a rare bird is
> > rare. It is when one is not looking,
> > at times one is not there
> > > that it comes.

As with bird-watching, glimpsing the divine requires waiting in silence. Absence and presence. But birds endure. 'Over millions of years they have kept to the flyways, many of them migrating thousands of miles with mysterious accuracy,' he has remarked. 'Their conquest of the air through flight has been achieved without any of the uproar and drain on Earth's resources with which man hurtles through space.' As well as condemnation of man, there is great admiration and love of birds in that last sentence.

Little tern

Peter Hughes

Chapter 11: Near the river: hinterland

This area is borderland. Usually I park my car just below Rhuddlan Castle, next to the church. Built in the thirteenth century, the castle still dominates not just the village and its by-pass. Five centuries later that redoubtable literary force Dr Johnson toured north Wales brimming with unenthusiasm but thought the castle 'a noble ruin', a sentiment shared by few Welsh people then or since. Moving mainly amongst anglicised squires and clerics, little wonder that he could write in 1774: 'Wales has nothing that can much excite or gratify curiosity. The mode of life is entirely English. I am glad I have seen it, though I have seen nothing because I now know that there is nothing to be seen.'

A century later came a much better-informed visitor. The poet Gerard Manley Hopkins, training for the priesthood at St Beuno's near Tremeirchion, wrote his most memorable sonnets in the Vale of Clwyd. One of them, 'The Sea and the Skylark', written in 1877, presents Rhyl in a familiar role as 'this shallow and frail town', symbol of 'our sordid turbid time'. But there was, there always is, another Rhyl. Angharad Llwyd, daughter of a Caerwys parson lived in Rhyl just a few years earlier. Essayist, genealogist, collector of subscriptions for Welsh books, she and her father who had accompanied Thomas Pennant on his travels had built a small museum of antiquities including a sword from Bosworth field. It's a Tudor link sustained today in Angharad Llwyd's house, Tŷ'n Rhyl, now a restaurant, Barratt's, featuring around its fireplace a fine carved bedhead. It once belonged to Gruffydd, a gentleman attendant to Catherine of Aragon, one of the wives of Henry VIII. Thick volumes in the National Library testify to Llwyd's work. As anglicisation swamped her class – she benefited from access to the libraries of the landed gentry – Angharad Llwyd determined to keep alive the flame of Welshness. As did Ieuan Glan Geirionydd, a Rhyl contemporary of hers, one of the most versatile Welsh poets of the nineteenth century.

Almost every feature of the landscape announces border country. Two other castles, or rather follies, visible from the river, Bodelwyddan and Gwrych, offer English versions of civility with the shaggy Carneddau looming behind. The writer of one of those weirdly enduring lines of verse – in this case, 'the boy stood on the burning deck' – was raised in a house on the Gwrych estate. Felicia Hemans, who was immensely popular in her day, wrote her best-known work while living in St Asaph between 1809 and 1825, including **Welsh Melodies** offering English versions of Welsh poems. Sir Walter Scott for one was not impressed: 'too many flowers and too little fruit'.

Such a strategic area crossed by a river near a border will inevitably have had a bloody history. Of the battle that stands out in local memory, the battle of Morfa Rhuddlan (*morfa*: salt-marsh) in the eighth century, apparently nothing was recorded or known before the late sixteenth century. But clearly it stirred the imagination, the story of King Offa's Saxons defeating Caradoc's army, killing all prisoners so the river ran red. Maybe that movingly tuneful air 'The Ballad of Morfa Rhuddlan' has contributed to the story's endurance. And it's a battle the writer Robert Graves recalls in his autobiographical record of World War I, **Goodbye to All That**. He records how, while stationed briefly near Rhyl with the Royal Welch Fusiliers in 1918, he heard of the death of Wilfred Owen amongst others: 'The news sent me walking out along the dyke above the marshes of Rhuddlan (an ancient battle, the Flodden of Wales), cursing and sobbing and thinking of the dead.' Of course Graves's knowledge of the battle was not some freak of circumstance. His father, Arthur Perceval, who published many Celtic songs and poems, had been made an honorary Gorsedd Bard at the Caernarfon National Eisteddfod in 1902. Robert Graves was to find his voice in the countryside around Harlech, and his first published poem was an English version of a Welsh *englyn*. He was on the border.

The river runs on, pulling in the country. To walk this section of the Clwyd is to hear echoes and feel vibrations though not all the literary voices are those of the dead. There's a poet and short story writer living in Rhuddlan represented in **The Penguin Book of Welsh Short Stories**. Glenda Beagan was born there, knows that what you

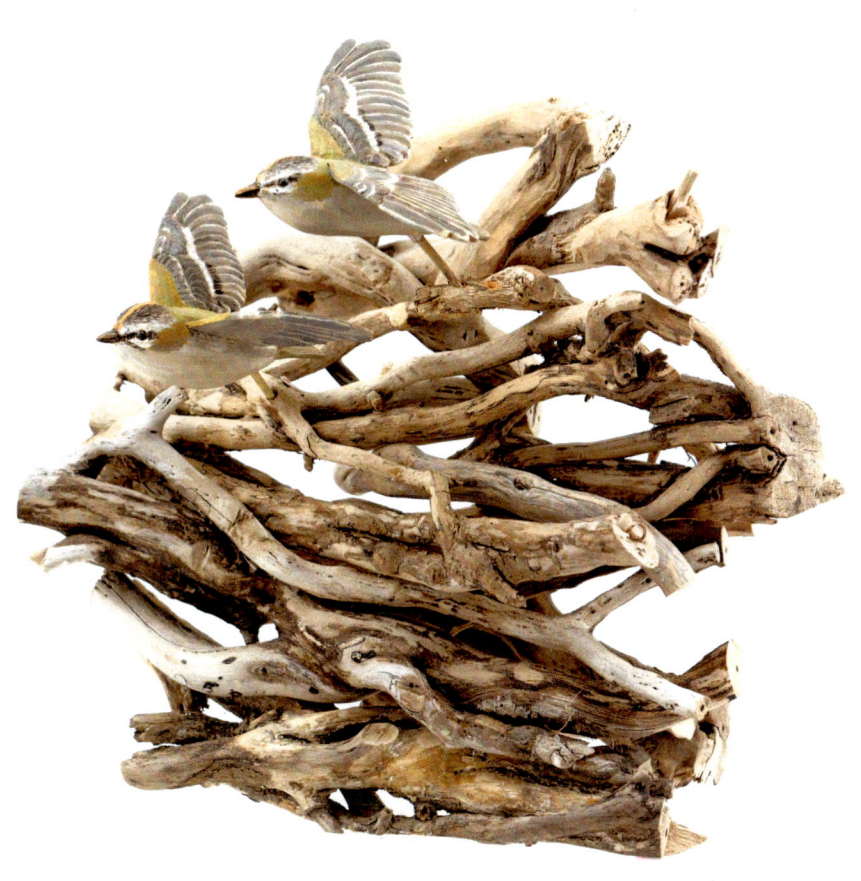

Firecrests on driftwood construction

Chris Porteous

Grasshopper warblers

Chris Porteous

have is where you are so the river runs strongly through her work. This is from a story called 'Seasonal Change':

> 'For centuries this track has led down to the ford, the only place to cross the river before the bridge was built. The first bridge. When was that? Twelfth century? She feels she is part of a pageant. An eighth century saint. A fourteenth century pilgrim. A Dominican hooded in black. Soldiers and statesmen. Footpads. Rogues. The folk of the land. The folk blurring and blending.'

It's just a three-mile stretch of river, hurrying past into the sea at Rhyl. There's so little to do or see apparently that the plot seems to thin. And it's open to the weather. It's a place where you'll meet joggers soundproofed against the seasons, canoeists and fishermen and, once, a flower-arranger poaching my driftwood. But I haven't mentioned yet the two towers visible from the river, that of St Asaph cathedral and also the Jubilee Tower above Ruthin, damaged in 1859 by the great storm that also wrecked the 'Royal Charter' and so brought Charles Dickens to Anglesey. What joins up hills is more than just the view.

Acknowledgements

Chapter 2
Tunnicliffe's Birds, Charles Tunnicliffe, Gollancz, 1984
Shorelands Summer Diary, Charles Tunnicliffe, Orbis, 1985
Memories of Mr and Mrs Harold Gill, article by Su Walls, Pwllheli (unpublished)
Dee Wildfowler, the last professional, a lifetime's recollections by Harold Gill of Parkgate (1883-1961), recorded and edited by Leslie Brockbank, 1982

Chapter 4
L T Ward & Bro.: Wildlife Counterfeiters, Byron Cheever, North American Decoys, a division of Hillcrest Publications Inc., PO Box 246, Spanish Fork, Utah 84660, 1970
The Decoy Duck, Bob Ridges, Dragon's World, 1988
Duck Decoys, Andrew Heaton, Shire Publications Ltd., 2001

Chapter 6
Skywalls, Clyde Holmes, Gwasg Carreg Gwalch, 1998
Variety of Men, C.P. Snow, Penguin Books, 1969

Chapter 7
Pierino's Snowdonia, Pierino Algieri, Gwasg Carreg Gwalch, 2013
Collected Poems 1945-1990, R.S. Thomas, J.M. Dent, 1991 ('Cynddylan on a Tractor')

Chapter 8
North by South, New and Selected Poems, John Davies, Seren, 2002

Chapter 9
The carved slates of Dyffryn Ogwen, National Museum of Wales, 1983
An Artist in the Quarries, Welsh Arts Council Touring Exhibition, 1981

Chapter 10
Collected Poems 1945 -1990, R.S. Thomas, J.M. Dent, 1991

With the exception of the three short poems by Clyde Holmes and my poems, all the quotations are brief and partial.